Buddha's Beat

Achieving Inner Peace Through Percussion

Table of Contents

Chapter 1. Introduction

Dive into a rhythmical journey like no other within the realms of our Special Report: Buddha's Beat: Achieving Inner Peace Through Percussion. Dancing between tranquil narratives and sonorous accounts, this exclusive guide explores an enlightening symbiosis of percussive music and Buddhist philosophies, aiming to aid in nurturing your inner well-being and long-drawn peace. Unshackle your daily stressors and find your inner harmony as we collectively drum towards tranquility. Ready for a mesmerizing mental retreat that tickles your senses and calms your soul? Beat the drum, let the rhythm flow, and come join us in this extraordinary adventure. You'd be surprised how a simple rhythm can create complex peace within your soul. Break away from the mundane and purchase this breathtaking Special Report today. We promise you; this is an odyssey worth embarking on!

Chapter 2. The Rhythm of Awakening: An Introduction to Percussive Meditation

In the vast world of music, percussive rhythms hold a special place, for they reflect the heartbeat of life, resonating within us like a primal echo. This chapter takes you on a journey - a rhythmic awakening - providing a comprehensive guide to achieving meditative harmony through percussive rhythms based on Buddhist philosophies.

2.1. The Pulse of Life

Percussion is an ancestral language, the oldest form of music in human history. The heart's pulsation is often seen as the primary percussion a human life encounters, laying a rhythmical foundation of our existence. Percussive sounds, whether manifested via drums, gongs, bells, or even the body, have been conduits for expressing emotions, telling stories, and creating bonds, intricately woven into the fabric of human culture and ritual. In many spiritual traditions, including Buddhism, percussive instruments have been used as tools for inducing altered states of consciousness, promoting focused concentration, and invoking a sense of unity.

2.2. Percussive Meditation: An Overview

Percussive Meditation blends the act of creating rhythmic sounds with mindful presence. Just as the rhythm of a drum can set the pace for a tune or guide a tribe's dance, percussive meditation can drive our inward journey, establishing a cadence for our thoughts and emotions. Defined by the synchronized beating of a percussive instrument, percussive meditation is all about harmonizing internal energy ('Chi', 'Prana') in accordance with the universe's rhythm. Its distinctive soundscapes can ease us into meditative states, quieting incessant mental chatter, and providing a fertile ground for self-exploration and internal equilibrium.

2.3. The Drum: A Gateway to Mindfulness

At the heart of percussive meditation is the drum, with its resonant beats providing a pathway to mindfulness. Every strike of the drumstick becomes an exercise in mindful presence, an opportunity to fully engage with the act of creating sound. The rhythm generated, both physically and acoustically, becomes the focus of our awareness. The drumming journey is not about the destination (or the perfect rhythm) but the process of rhythmic creation and absorption, in which the drummer becomes the drummed, and the sound becomes the silenced.

2.4. The Buddhist Philosophy of Mindfulness

Central to Buddhist philosophy is the practice of mindfulness, defined as open, non-judgmental attention to present-moment experiences. By bringing the mind to the present moment, we liberate ourselves from the burdens of past regrets and future anxieties. The beauty of percussive meditation lies in its ability to integrate this Buddhist philosophy with the act of producing and absorbing rhythmic sound, making music creation a mindfulness practice.

Mindful drumming is an embodiment of the essential Buddhist teachings of impermanence, non-self, and suffering. It allows us to observe how sound arises and passes away, demonstrating impermanence. It shows us that there is no self within the sound, pointing to the notion of non-self. Lastly, as we absorb the rhythms, making peace with each resonant noise, we learn to embrace suffering and slowly let it go.

2.5. The Power of Vibration

Sound is essentially vibration, and different frequencies of vibration can significantly impact our mental and emotional states. When we strike a drum, we rise with its rhythms, our vibrations align with the percussive beats, causing a state of resonance – where the internal meets the external. This resonance can eventually lead to a state of 'entrainment', in which our brain waves, heart rate, and respiration sync with the drum's rhythms, cultivating a profound state of relaxation and focused awareness.

2.6. Crafting Your Percussive Meditation

As you venture into the realm of percussive meditation, remember this: there's no right or wrong beat. The purpose is not just to make music, but to 'be with' the music, to stand in the uninterrupted flow of rhythm and vibration, and to fully embrace the present moment. Start by focusing on each beat. Observe the sensation in your hands as they strike the drum, listen to the sound produced simultaneously, and take note of your feelings. Over time, as your mindfulness deepens, you'll begin to feel a sense of attunement with the rhythm, a sensation of oneness with the universe.

2.7. Conclusion: A Symphony of Serenity

The rhythm of awakening is a unique journey, an intimate dance with the present moment orchestrated through the drum's beat. As you strike the drum mindfully, as you listen to each sound arise and fade away, you are not merely drumming; you're connecting to an ancient tradition, embarking on a meditative voyage, and becoming a part of a universal rhythm. It's through this journey into sound that we resonate with our true selves, discover our inner peace, and cultivate an experience of serenity.

Percussive meditation, grounded in Buddhist philosophies, promises to be a mesmerizing voyage of awakening. As you journey on, remember: It's not just playing the drum; it's realizing the drum within you. And within these beats lies your path to inner peace and tranquillity.

Chapter 3. Sounding The Zen: History of Percussion in Buddhism

From its inception, Buddhism and music have been inextricably linked, with the sound of percussion interwoven delicately into the practice's rich tapestry of ritual and philosophy. The history of percussion in Buddhism is as varied and multi-layered as the practice itself, moving alongside the evolution of thought and providing the transcendental beats that have guided millions to discover and explore the depths of their own existence.

3.1. Building the Beat: The Use of Percussion Instruments in Early Buddhism

The role of the beat, particularly as produced by percussion instruments, has played a significant part in the development and progression of Buddhist tradition. The primal pulse of percussive sounds flows through many rites and rituals, symbolizing and calling out to the innate rhythm of life itself.

In early Buddhism, which emerged around the 5th century B.C.E., percussion instruments were incorporated into religious ceremonies as a means of guiding monks and followers to achieve a harmonious mental state. The beat of the drum or the clear toll of the bell signified the beginning and end of meditation sessions, providing markers in the otherwise timeless expanse of contemplation.

Certain types of percussion instruments were especially significant in early Buddhism. The Muyu, or wooden fish, had deep metaphorical resonance. This hollow wooden percussion instrument, often shaped like a fish, was tapped rhythmically as a reminder of innate wakefulness that one should not let their spiritual discipline slip into unconsciousness, much like how a fish never closes its eyes.

3.2. Sound Waves: Branching Buddhism and the Evolution of Percussion

As Buddhism diffused from its homeland of India and into the neighboring countries of China, Japan, Korea, and Southeast Asia, so did its percussive practices. These new take-ups of Buddhism both embraced pre-existing instruments and inspired the creation of new forms.

China witnessed the evolution of Buddhist gongs, bells, and drums that were used in monastic ceremonies and larger ritualistic events. Japan became known for its Mokugyo, a wooden percussion instrument similar but distinct from its Chinese counterpart. In Korea, the temple block called Mokeo became a pivotal instrument, echoing throughout temples and monasteries, marking time, signaling gatherings, and punctuating chants.

Each new branch of Buddhism created a symphony that reverberated with its unique tonality, enriched by the beating heart of percussion. This rhythmic diversity led to a broad and colorful palette of sacred sounds that, while uniquely individual, united in their purpose to facilitate enlightenment and guide spiritual reflection.

3.3. The Deep Rooted Drum: Buddhist Drumming

Buddhist percussion must also pay tribute to the drum's deep-seated roots in its religious traditions, particularly in Tibetan Buddhism. The Damaru or the Tibetan hand-drum, often held in the hand of wrathful deities and yogis in meditative practice, symbolizes the impermanent nature of all things. As the drum is played, it emulates the heartbeat, reminding practicers of their own transience.

The traditional Tibetan ritual drum, or Ngoma drum, also plays a crucial role. Its dual faces are said to represent compassion and wisdom—two essential Buddhist virtues. Beating this drum allows one to align with these virtues, making it an active form of prayer and an integral part of the ceremonious dance known as Cham.

3.4. Sacred Sounds: The Harmonious Philosophy of Buddhist Percussion

The philosophy behind Buddhist percussion goes beyond mere instrumental practice. It is deeply entwined with the belief in the power of resonance to harmonize a person's spiritual energy. The act of striking a drum or tolling a bell is not simply about producing sound but about creating vibrations that can affect a person's mental and spiritual state.

Buddhist teachings highlight the use of rhythmic repetition to provide a pathway to meditation, with the consistent beat of a drum or bell serving as an auditory guide toward tranquility and enlightenment. Each beat is an invitation to let go of worldly concerns and delve deeper into personal existence, to the purest form of consciousness.

In conclusion, the history of percussion in Buddhism is as

rhythmically diverse as it is spiritually profound. From the initial use of basic percussive instruments in early Buddhism to the evolution of percussion traditions as Buddhism spread across Asia, the beat has always served as a guiding force. The harmonious blend of rhythm, music, and spirituality evident in Buddhist percussion reflects the broader wisdom of Buddhist philosophy—providing a pathway to inner peace and rhythmic inward journey, one beat at a time.

Chapter 4. Drumming to Serenity: Techniques in Percussive Meditation

The beauty of percussive meditation lies within its deceptive simplicity. However, the more the technique is practiced, the more you would realize, its potential stretches out far beyond a mere rhythmic production on a percussive instrument. The beating drum can act as an echo of our hearts, the rumbling bass subtly mirroring our inherent vibrations. Let's dive right into this rich landscape of percussive meditation, unfolding its depths, and exploring its practices in detail.

4.1. The Rhythm of the Mind

Every beat of the drum is a rhythmic crest on the serene sea of our consciousness. As the rhythm repeats, it creates a mantra, guiding us towards a deep, meditative state that promotes both physical relaxation and mental clarity.

The first step in percussive meditation is selecting your instrument. While the drum is the most recognized tool for this practice, other percussive instruments can also provide the same serene effects. These could be cymbals, tambourines, gongs, bells, xylophones, marimbas, or even the human body itself through hand clapping or foot stomping. Your choice should resonate with your preferences, comfort, and the sound that helps you reach a state of deep relaxation.

Once you've selected your instrument, find a comfortable, quiet place where you won't be disturbed. Settle into a comfortable posture. Many practitioners prefer sitting cross-legged on a meditation mat, but you can also lean against a wall or sit in a chair. The goal is physical comfort so that your body doesn't distract your mind during the practice.

4.2. The Beat of Being

To begin your percussive meditation, start by taking a few deep breaths. Immerse your senses in the environment around you, but focus your attention inwardly - in tune with your heartbeat. Feel the life within you rhythmic and divine.

Slowly, gently, start producing a simple beat on your chosen instrument. This beat should mirror your heart – steady, rhythmic, and unobtrusive. Allow yourself to get lost in the simplicity of the rhythm. As you continue, you may start to notice the resounding beats aligning with the rhythm of your heartbeat.

4.3. Empowering Resonance

Gradually, intensify the rhythm; make it slightly faster or louder. The change in rhythm is symbolic of our ever-changing circumstances and emotions. Despite the changing rhythm, continue to keep your mind tranquil, observing the fluctuations but not getting carried away. This practice in mindfulness allows us to develop a deeper awareness of our inner state and teaches us to manage our reactions towards the constant changes in life.

Once you feel familiarized with the changing rhythms, start experimenting with different patterns. Creating a new rhythm helps us tap into our creative thinking, encouraging a dynamic flow of thoughts. Experiment with different beats, tapping into your creativity and imagination.

4.4. The Transcendence of Tempo

However, always remember, there is no right or wrong rhythm when it comes to percussive meditation. The goal is to use the rhythm to anchor your mind, to absorb your full attention, allowing external distractions to dim and internal chatter to settle.

As you progress in your practice, you may begin integrating more complex rhythms or even adding other instruments. Try integrating different rhythms together, or shifting between different rhythms in the same meditation session, manifesting the ebb and flow of life, with its ever-changing, unpredictable nature. Observe how your mind reacts to these changes and transitions, training it to remain steady and composed through life's metaphorical rhythm changes.

4.5. The Harmonic Homecoming

Remember to conclude your meditative session gently. Slow down the rhythm gradually, tracing your journey back to the steady thumping beat that you started with. As the sound around you fades away, sit silently, absorbing the tranquility and the residual vibrations in your surroundings and within you. Take a few deep, full breaths, allowing yourself to feel grounded again and bring your conscious attention back to the world before opening your eyes.

The repetitive percussion brings us to a profound state of consciousness. This meditative form can be personalized to each individual's rhythm, creating a unique symphony of serenity. Whether you are a seasoned meditation practitioner or just a beginner, give percussive meditation a try. The rhythmic journey might lead you to unforeseen depths of peace and enlightenment within yourself. Like a rhythmic wave, let the percussive meditation carry you towards a shore of serenity.

Remember, every journey begins with a single step, or in our case, a gentle tap on a drum. So, pick up your instrument, discover your rhythm, and embark on your percussive meditation journey today. May the rhythm guide you to inner peace and tranquillity.

Practice makes perfect, and as you continue your percussive meditation journey, you might discover your unique rhythm that echoes your inner self, embracing serenity with every beat. Embrace the silence between the beats as they represent the empty spaces in life – recognizing them is as crucial as acknowledging the existence of the beats. Percussive meditation, at its core, reflects life itself - a rhythmic interplay of beats and silences.

As you delve into the practice, you'll find a supportive community of fellow percussionists and meditators, offering not just instruction and guidance, but also a shared sense of journey and discovery. There's a world of rhythm out there waiting for you. Get out there and find your beat.

Chapter 5. The Tao of Tone: Understanding the Impact of Different Sounds on the Mind

In the grand odyssey of self-discovery and peace, no pathway is as vibrant and engaging as the exploration of auditive landscapes. Percussive music, with its intricate web of rhythms and beats, bears a fascinating link to our mental and emotional well-being, heightened exponentially when adjoined to Buddhist philosophies. Complex, you imagine? Let's delve into it.

5.1. Discerning Beats and Brainwaves

Sound is a physical force - one that can alter our state of mind significantly. Percussive rhythms, in particular, have a way of summoning our intrinsic connection to the world. How do these beats cause such profound impacts on the mind? Let's untangle this mystery.

Each sound carries its own unique frequency. Think of the diverse patterns you can detect in a heart monitor, each representing the beat of the heart. Similarly, the brain also has a rhythmic quality, known as brain waves, which can be classified into five different types—Delta, Theta, Alpha, Beta, and Gamma.

Research suggests a powerful symbiosis between these brainwaves and the rhythms that reach our ears. Slow beats, like that of a ceremonial drum, can provoke the Delta waves (0.5 to 3 Hz), associated with deep dreamless sleep and restoration. Medium-paced beats may induce Alpha waves (8 to 12 Hz), which underlie our states of relaxation and calm imagination. Faster, upbeat rhythms trigger

Beta waves (12 to 30 Hz), often linked to waking consciousness and logical thinking.

5.2. The Resonance of Percussion

Buddhist philosophy attaches profound significance to resonance – or the vibrant hum of all things in the universe. The science of Cymatics shows how sounds, including percussive beats, create distinctive vibrational patterns. These patterns can be observed in a variety of mediums, including sand, water, and even the human body.

Different percussion instruments produce unique sonic landscapes. A deep, low beat from a frame drum creates broad, slow-moving patterns – resembling the gradual flow of continental plates. Comparatively, higher-frequency sounds, like those from a djembe or tambourine, create tighter, more complex patterns, similar to diverse ecosystems.

The practice of mindful drumming involves not just playing these instruments but immersing oneself in their resonance, embodying these patterns, and harmonizing with the universal frequencies.

5.3. The Healing Properties of Percussive Sounds

For centuries, people across the globe, spanning different cultures and spiritual tenets, have used percussive music and rhythmic sounds for healing and spiritual exploration.

Evidence from neuroscientific research reinforces the therapeutic effect of drumming and its ability to reduce anxiety, lower blood pressure, and instill a sense of well-being. A research study at Stanford University found that even 30 minutes of rhythmic drumming could induce an Alpha brain wave state, similar to the deep relaxation achieved through meditation.

In the Buddhist context, percussive sounds are not just potent healers but also profound teachers. They reinforce the teachings of impermanence (anicca), dissipation (anatta), and suffering (dukkha) - the fundamental building blocks of Buddhist philosophy. As each beat strikes and fades away, it mirrors the transient nature of life, giving listeners a palpable experience of these core teachings.

5.4. An Expressive Outlet

The beauty of percussive music is that it offers an expressive outlet and connects individuals on a deeper level. The shared experience of producing and immersing in rhythmic sounds fosters enhanced interpersonal relationships and communal unity – generating a collective wave of tranquility.

Famed Buddhist monk and peace activist, Thich Nhat Hanh, has famously quoted, "The most precious gift we can offer others is our presence." Fostering presence and mindfulness is at the heart of percussive music – every beat demands your attention, brings you into the moment, and connects you intimately with the world around you.

5.5. Setting the Mood for Meditation

Percussion offers an accessible and immediate pathway to meditative states. The simple act of attentive listening or playing can mirror a meditation practice. Essentially, the drum beat becomes the focus of our awareness. Like the breath in mindfulness meditation, it anchors the wandering mind to the present moment, to this place and time.

By understanding the influence that varying percussive sounds can have on our emotional and mental states, we can utilize rhythms as a form of 'tonic' – with different beats acting as catalysts to evoke desired moods or mental states. Hence, the meditative practice aligns with the philosophy of the Middle Way – not too hard, not too soft, harmoniously centered.

To say it simply, the Tao of Tone is about understanding the intrinsic relationship between rhythm and mind. Be it for healing, understanding impermanence, fostering community, or setting the stage for meditation, percussive sounds are guides on the journey towards inner peace and tranquility.

Whether you are a musician, a meditation enthusiast, or an explorer on the journey to inner peace, understanding the Tao of Tone can offer you a richer, fuller experience. So, pick your drum, empty your mind, listen to the beats, and patently witness how the rhythms dance in the vast expanse of your consciousness. You'd realize that in the end, this vibrant palette of beats paints nothing but peace.

Chapter 6. Mindful Beats: Applying Buddhist Teachings to Percussive Practice

Practicing mindfulness involves bringing one's attention to experiences occurring in the present moment without judgment. Within Buddhism, it is a part of the spiritual path towards enlightenment. As we embark on this chapter, we will explore the intertwining journey of mindfulness and percussion, guiding you towards an innovative path of inner peace and tranquility.

6.1. Understanding Mindfulness in Buddhism

Mindfulness, or 'sati' in Pali, a language of ancient Indian Buddhist texts, is a significant element of the Noble Eightfold Path proposed by Buddha to cease suffering ('Dukkha'). Yet this path is not merely an escape from suffering; it's a guide towards the ultimate joy, genuine happiness, and enlightened understanding.

Buddha teaches us the importance of staying anchored in the present moment. Instead of getting tangled in the past's regrets or the future's anxious anticipations, he emphasized the essence of acknowledging current reality as it is: a perpetual flow of changing conditions.

6.2. The Magic of Percussive Practice

The art of percussion is strikingly similar to the philosophy of mindfulness. Percussion, in essence, is the practice of creating sound through touch - it involves striking, scraping, shaking, or any other similar techniques. It conjures an array of feelings, from the pulsating throb of a drum to the subtle whisper of a brush against a cymbal.

One can argue that percussion, in its totality, is a form of meditation. It promotes attention to the present moment by focusing on the formation of sound. It also allows for self-expression and the release of pent-up emotions, serving as an effective stress reliever.

Drumming, the most popular form of percussion, builds coordination and rhythm, both of which are vital not just in music but also in the pulsating beat of life itself. It generates vibrations that can have a synchronization effect on our bodies, denoting that rhythm, much like nature, is inherent in us.

6.3. Synchronizing Mindfulness and Percussion

The fusion of mindfulness and percussion offers a fascinating approach - much like a drum that produces diverse sounds based on how it's struck, our mind generates various thoughts based on the stimuli it receives.

As we practice mindfulness through percussive technique, we need to pay total attention to the drum's onset, course, and termination of each beat. We learn to become absorbed in the 'now' and acknowledge each sensation as it emerges. The focus on individual notes helps us to apply the same focus to our thoughts, allowing us to stay rooted in the reality of the present moment.

Likewise, playing a drum rhythm requires us to maintain a steady pace over time. This steadiness mirrors the Buddhist philosophy of the 'Middle Way'- a balanced approach to life that avoids extremes and seeks harmony between opposing forces.

6.4. Mindful Drumming: A Step-by-Step Guide

1. **Setting the Scene:** Choose a quiet, comfortable space where you can perform your percussive practice uninterrupted. Arrange your session at a time when you can dedicate your full concentration to it. Familiarize yourself with your drum - understand the sounds it produces and how it reacts to different types of touches.

2. **Starting the Rhythm:** Begin by tapping your drum lightly with your fingers. Pay careful attention to the sounds produced. Observe how the sound resonates and then fades away.

3. **Paying Attention:** As you continue to tap the drum, focus your attention on the sensation created. Listen carefully to the sound patterns. Pay attention to how your body feels. Do you notice a change in your heartbeat? Your breathing?

4. **Keeping the Balance:** Maintain a steady rhythm. Just as it's essential to balance our lives, it's crucial to balance our rhythm too. Avoid getting too fast or too slow; maintain the 'middle path'.

5. **Responding, not Reacting:** If your mind starts to wander, gently bring it back to the sounds. Resist the urge to hit the drum harder or mute it completely. Instead, respond to the wanderings in your mind by adjusting your rhythm - making it quieter or louder, faster, or slower.

6. **Visualizing the Sound:** This is an optional step, but it might help some people. As you progress, visualize the sound as a visible entity traveling outward from the drum, filling the room, and finally dissolving into silence. This is an exercise that connects us more deeply to our environment and encourages respect for the spaces we inhabit.

Through this practice, you develop an understanding of the richness of the relationship between mindfulness and percussion. As you successfully master the state of focused calm, you take a significant stride closer to achieving initial peace and well-being.

6.5. Finding Inner Peace through Percussive Tranquility

When practicing mindful percussion, you are taking control of your attention and directing it in a structured, rhythmic manner. This is exceptionally therapeutic as it helps regulate our emotional state, foster relaxation, and unwind the often-overlooked stress stored in our bodies.

With consistent practice, percussion can stimulate a reconnection between the mind and body, unveiling a profound sense of inner peace—a sense that aligns well with the core Buddhist belief in the interconnectedness of all things.

In our modern era of distractions, finding an immersive, engaging practice that helps us root ourselves back in the beauty of the present moment is truly precious. Combining mindfulness with the rhythmic, resonating beauty of percussion can provide us with such a practice—an enlightening journey that possibly brings us one small step closer to the profound wisdom of Buddhism. Let the rhythm lead your voyage to tranquility; after all, the beat of the drum is not far different from the beat of our hearts.

Chapter 7. Striking Balance: Symbiosis of Rhythm and Silence

Percussive music, intrinsically tied to the rhythm of life, mirrors the essential teachings of Buddhism, just as silence embodies the allure of void, calling us towards exploration. This perspective of sound and silence culminates into a profound union which we shall explore in depth.

7.1. The Rhythm of Life: A Buddhist Perspective

The Buddhist philosophy is notable for its profound observations about life, among which it draws parallels between life's rhythm and the teachings transmitted. Life, like percussive music, is based on rhythm — a series of events that unfold in a regular, predictable pattern. It's a resonance found not only in nature's grand design but also within our inner biological cycles.

One's heartbeat, the cadence of breath, the circadian rhythm of sleep and wakefulness — all these undulate in a rhythm that anchors our lives. They are life-perpetuating rhythms, reflective of universal truths which offer us deep insights into the workings of 'Dukkha' (suffering), 'Anicca' (impermanence), and 'Anatta' (non-self) — the core tenets of Buddhism.

Through a rhythmic exploration of these tenets, Buddhists cultivate mindfulness - an understanding of the present moment and its sufficiency. Just as each drum beat is experienced in singularity without anticipating the next, every moment in life should be seen as complete, not being attached to the past or future.

7.2. Drumming: A Pathway to Spiritual Awakening

Buddhist culture leverages the enigmatic power of percussive music to delve into a spiritual journey. The mindful act of drumming becomes a form of meditation. Each strike of the drumstick, each resonating sound wave, becomes a pathway leading towards inner peacefulness and harmony.

The drummer's concentrated movements and the perceptible rhythmic progression create a trance-like state, helping to awaken heightened awareness. It elevates the practitioner's consciousness, forging a connection with the metaphysical realm. The soul of the drummer becomes the listener, the creator, and the music itself - a harmonious, unmuddled state of being.

7.3. Embracing the Sound of Silence

With all the enchantment attributed to rhythm, we must equally place emphasis on silence. As resonant drumbeats create earthly rhythm, silent intervals sculpt the shape and contour of the whole performance. Just as rhythms are necessary to experience music, silence is necessary to experience peace.

In Buddhism, silence is synonymous with the concept of 'Shunyata' — emptiness. It implies an openness or readiness to receive, devoid of preconceived notions or biases. Silence is a junction where the clamor of thoughts is stilled, making way for serene introspection and revelation.

In a percussive performance, the silences, or rests, define the rhythm as much as the strikes themselves. The resultant interplay leads to a harmonious, enriching symphony signifying the oscillation between being and non-being, echoing the Buddhist belief in the cycle of life and death - rebirth and cessation.

7.4. Creating Harmony: A Dance Between Rhythm and Silence

Through a rhythmic dance, Buddhism speaks to the profound depth of life and the pathway to attain inner peace. Drums signal a rhythm, while silence punctuates it, the two elements together forming the symphony of existence.

Just as we cannot observe light without experiencing dark, a rhythm is incomplete without the essence of silence. This delicate balance intertwines in percussive music, where drumbeats bring forth the existence, and silent intervals reveal the vacuum. The resulting symphony represents a harmonious coexistence, epitomizing the Middle Way in Buddhism.

In adapting to the rhythmic symphony of life, one can develop equanimity, the quality of being unruffled by the highs and lows, just as a seasoned drummer remains unperturbed when transitioning between sound and silence in a piece of music. The rhythm brings excitement and energy to life, while the silence aids in introspection, balance, and renewal.

Through the exploration of rhythm and silence, the symbiosis of both provides a rewarding journey towards personal growth and enlightenment. By harnessing their energies, you gain vitality from the rhythm, tranquility from the silence, thus achieving the ultimate state of balanced peace.

By the end of this exploration, one realizes that the teachings of Buddhism and the intrinsic elements of percussive music aren't far apart. Both encompass life and the universe's fundamental aspects - rhythm and silence, birth and cessation, sound and void. This understanding forms an ethereal connection, bridging the gap between the spiritual self and the mundane existence, inevitably aiding in achieving inner peace.

Chapter 8. Inner Symphony: The Healing Power of Percussion

Just as the dawn breaks to the symphony of birds telling the world that a new day has begun, our inner self also responds to the rhythmic beat of the heart, providing a tempo for our life and impacting our emotional state in unimaginable ways. This chapter delves into the healing power of percussion, illuminating its profound influence on our psyche and connection to Buddhist philosophies of inner peace.

8.1. A Heartbeat Away

The healing power of percussive music begins at the moment of conception, with an unborn child first experiencing the rhythm of their mother's heartbeat. This ambient symphony dictates our very perception of life; it is the first rhythm we accommodate, making it an ingrained part of our existence.

Listening to percussion can guide our internal rhythms back to this comforting tempo. The primal nature of drums connects us to the visceral aspect of our existence, which can induce a calming effect that allows us to connect deeper with our inner selves.

8.2. The History of Healing Drums

Drumming has been an integral part of human civilization for millennia. Ancient cultures recognized the healing potential of rhythmic drumming and incorporated it within their rituals and ceremonies. Whether it is the Shamanic tribes of Siberia, the indigenous cultures of America, or the serene monks in Tibetan monasteries, each utilized percussion as a tool of enlightenment and healing.

Buddhism, in particular, has given rhythmic practices a spiritual significance, aligning the rhythmic beating with the pulse of the universe. This confluence of inner rhythm and cosmic rhythm brings about a tranquil state of mind that aids in meditation and introspective self-discovery.

8.3. Sound and Vibrations: The Physical Response

Scientifically, the therapeutic effect of rhythmic percussion can be attributed to the vibrations that drums produce. These vibrations resonate through our bodies, affecting our cells on a molecular level.

When a drum is struck, the skin vibrates and sends ripples outwards. Similar to our eardrum that vibrates in response to sound waves, our bodies react to these waves by creating a 'resonance' or 'entrainment' where our internal rhythms align with these external frequencies. This alignment stimulates areas of the brain responsible for feelings of tranquility, thus activating our natural distressing mechanisms.

8.4. Neurological Impact of Percussion

The rhythmic pulsations of the drums stimulate the brain in ways that few other instruments can. It promotes the release of endorphins, the body's natural mood enhancers, and slows down our brain waves to a relaxed theta state, promoting enhanced cognitive functions and reducing stress. Moreover, percussion helps synchronize the cerebral hemispheres. This synchronization boosts creativity, intuition, and holistic thinking by getting the 'thinking' (left brain) and 'feeling' (right brain) in harmony.

8.5. Drum Circles: Collective Catharsis

Drum circles, or group drumming, add another layer to the healing properties of percussion; the aspect of communal interaction. Participating in a drum circle empowers individuals to contribute to a collective rhythm, nurturing a sense of belonging and connectivity.

This rhythmic unity acts as a metaphor for the interconnectedness of all beings. The collective beat of the drum mirrors the collective heartbeat of humanity, further reinforcing Buddha's teachings of community and interdependence.

8.6. Personal Drumming: The Meditative State

Private drumming sessions can be equally profound. As the rhythms begin to flow, the drummer embarks on a journey inwards, reaching into the deepest recesses of the self to uncover hidden growth areas.

Buddhists often use drumming as a meditative practice to drown out external distractions, allowing them to enter the peaceful mind state required for deep inner exploration. The steady beat serves as a reference point, helping to anchor the wandering mind and guide it back to the present moment.

8.7. A Beat Away From Inner Peace

At its core, percussion is a gateway to inner peace. Its innate ability to cross the barriers of the conscious mind and reach into the psyche makes it an invaluable tool for achieving zen. As each drum beat resonates through our being, it serves as a reminder of our connection to life's essential rhythm, the heartbeat of the universe.

Percussion opens us up to a world within us seldom explored, facilitating the journey towards self-actualization. By synchronizing our thoughts, feelings, and consciousness to the rhythm, we can gradually unshackle the mind from internal conflict and find harmony and tranquility within our inner symphony.

Embarking on this rhythmic journey may seem daunting, but it's never too late to pick up the drumsticks. After all, isn't rhythm something that has been beating in our hearts since inception? So, take a step, beat the drum, feel the rhythm and let the inner symphony play its harmonious notes. Embrace the tranquility, the connectivity, and the rhythm of life.

Chapter 9. Sacred Sounds: Exploring the Instruments of Buddhist Percussion

In the heart of our exploration, we focus on the instrumental assortment, an intrinsic aspect weaving an integral part of the aural tapestry of Buddhist temple rituals. These sonic tools, etched out of wood, brass, and other earthly materials, are more than mere musical instruments in the Buddhist context. They imbue spiritual symbolism and merit reverence, each boasting remarkable qualities that culminate in creating various resonances, ripples of serenity echoing within and around us.

9.1. Traversing the Sonic Spectrum: An Overview

Among the wide array of percussive instruments that echo the Buddhist faith, perhaps the most prevalent consists of the Dhyangro, Moktak, Singing Bowls, and the Damaru. Their distinct tones, borne out of different materials and techniques, collectively create an awe-inspiring journey through the sensory spectrum of sound, nudging us into realms of peace and tranquility.

To begin our exploration, let us approach each of these instruments individually, delving deep into historical context, symbolic interpretations, and the mesmerizing workings behind their soothing sonority.

9.2. The Dhyangro: Echoes of Ancestral Invocation

The Dhyangro, primarily known to the Shamanic rituals of Nepal, reflects a resounding link to Buddhism. Categorized as a frame drum, it comprises two fundamental components: wood-carved handle symbolizing the thunderbolt (vajra) and a round frame covered with a thin layer of animal skin, evoking our primordial union with nature.

In its construction alone, the Dhyangro encodes deep layers of symbolic interpretation. The wooden vajra handle epitomizes the stability of spirit, akin to the unwavering force of thunder. On the other hand, the drum head, resounding with echoes of ancestral lineage, acts as a bridge between primal instinct and, ultimately, our quest for enlightenment.

Whether struck with a curved beater or simply shivered to a shamanic rhythm, the Dhyangro sends out a potent reverberation felt deeply within our psyche, nudging us towards a profound sense of interconnection.

9.3. The Moktak: Wooden Waves of Mindfulness

Next, we steer our exploration towards the wooden instrument of mindfulness - the Moktak. Revered by Asian Buddhist monks, the Moktak, or wooden fish, is an essential percussive pulse during sutra chanting and other temple rituals.

Carved from solid wood into a fish body outline, the Moktak strikes with a hollow thud, awakening the mind towards a state of heightened alertness. Its distinct sound serves as a subtle reminder that, just like fish never close their eyes, monks should maintain perpetual mindfulness in their spiritual pursuit.

Moktak's heartening influence is not strictly isolated to monastic circles. Besotted by its tranquil resonance, many contemporary practitioners readily involve Moktak in daily meditation routines, revealing the boundless reach of this instrument.

9.4. Singing Bowls: Symphony of Resonant Calm

No exploration of Buddhist soundscapes could be comprehensive without the mention of the enchanting Singing Bowls. Originating from the Himalayan regions, these bowls, usually made of seven different metals, are an epitome of harmony in a physical form.

Struck lightly or played with a wooden mallet moving along their rim, Singing Bowls unveil a harmonious symphony entrancing us into a state of resonant calm. This serene tranquility is believed to align with our vibrational frequencies, aiding deep meditation and therapeutic healing.

Indeed, the calming vibrations emitted by these bowls have seen their rapid adaption into modern therapeutic techniques, reiterating their timeless appeal.

9.5. The Damaru: Rhythmic Resounding of Impermance

Finally, bringing our exploration to an impactful conclusion, we find ourselves in the pulsating presence of Damaru – a small, two-headed drum, traditionally made from the skulls of small creatures. Primarily employed in Tibetan rituals, the Damaru, with its rhythmic tremors, symbolizes the impermanence of life and resoundingly echoes the Buddhist philosophy of transience.

Despite their seemingly macabre construction, Damarus are not instruments of intimidation but tools of enlightenment. Rotated swiftly between the palms, their percussive beats echo the transient nature of life, encouraging practitioners to acknowledge and appreciate the fleeting beauty of existence.

9.6. Drawing Conclusions: An Aural Canvas ushering Serenity

Enveloping us with their distinctive soundscapes, these percussive tools of Buddhist rituals indeed hold transformative abilities. Transcending the mere physical, each stroke, beat, and harmony ignites our senses, ushering us towards a profound serenity aligned with the philosophy of Buddhism.

To fully comprehend the depth of these instruments, one must immerse oneself in their resonance. Only then can we decipher the unsaid and maybe catch a fleeting glimpse of the deeper truth that lies beneath the realm of worldly noise. Only then can we render our internal chaos to silence, suturing our souls with the serene symphony of peaceful percussion.

Chapter 10. Rhythmical Mindfulness: A Guide to Daily Percussive Practice

In a world that continually pulls us in numerous directions, it becomes crucial for us to find an anchor - a constant rhythm that aligns our inner chaos into a peaceful symphony. Percussive music intertwines this rhythmic anchor with mindful practice, allowing you to cultivate a tranquil frame of mind amidst the chaos that graces daily life.

10.1. The Power of Percussion

Percussive instruments are not merely tools for creating rhythm but are conduits of emotional expression. The simplicity of rhythm belies its profound ability to ground us in the present moment and foster connection with ourselves. This, coupled with the focused attention required to play, initiates a mechanism similar to meditation. You bare yourself in time, rhythm, and vibration, grounding your awareness in the current moment, deepening your connection to your inherent calm.

No matter how intricate or uncomplicated the rhythm, each beat serves to guide us towards our inner self. Absorbed in this rhythmic journey, we begin to experience an unparalleled awakening, a musically induced phenomenon where the mind amplifies its focus into the present.

10.2. Cultivating Mindfulness through Rhythm

Delving into the heart of rhythm demands comfort in the realm of uncertainty. One must allow the rhythm to guide while attentively falling into step with its pattern. In this way, you deliberately cultivate mindfulness, attuning your awareness to the rhythm's ebb and flow. Every beat becomes an invitation to deepen your connection to the present moment.

Embodied in this practice are the pillars of mindfulness: present moment awareness, non-judgment, open curiosity, and patience. Mindfulness dissolves the imaginary boundaries between the self and the rhythm, blurring the lines between experiencing and listening to forge a palpable connection.

10.3. Techniques for Daily Rhythm Practice

A daily percussive practice involves both the physical and mental aspects of rhythm. Here are some methods to incorporate into your daily rhythm routine:

1. **Body Percussion:** This involves using your body to create rhythm. Finger snaps, hand claps, thigh slaps - the possibilities are endless. This practice aids you in becoming acquainted with rhythm, and further enhances your mindfulness.

2. **Meditative Drumming:** Aim for a tranquil rhythm and allow your mind to meld with the beat. The drumming provides a focus point for your mindfulness as you let the bombardment of daily thoughts fade into the peripheral.

For both techniques, start off simple. Accept the rhythm as it comes, without forcing changes or expecting outcomes.

Tips:

- Be patient. It's less about mastering a beat and more about surrendering to the rhythm.

- Experiment with different instruments. Explore various timbres and sound patterns.

- Create a dedicated space and time for practice to help reinforce the discipline of mindfulness.

10.4. The Rewards of Rhythmical Mindfulness

When we venture into this rhythmical realm of mindfulness, we unlock an opportunity to observe, inquire, and reflect on our thoughts and emotions. This rhythm-induced mindfulness allows us to engage with our inner state without needlessly clinging to it.

Simultaneously, the rhythmic repetition cultivates a sense of inner tranquility, infusing our mindfulness practice with an experience of harmony and peace. As we weave mindfulness and rhythm together, we often gain invaluable insights, attain clarity, and nurture a more profound sense of self-awareness. Ultimately, rhythmical mindfulness creates a space where consciousness can emerge and flourish beyond the cacophony of everyday life.

10.5. A Symphony of Inner Peace

In the end, rhythmical mindfulness is not merely about learning an instrument or perfecting a beat. It's about unearthing of a new language, a rhythmic language of serenity and awareness. It's about discovering your own symphony of inner peace amidst the disarray of daily life - one drumbeat at a time.

As you continue this mindful rhythmic journey, you begin to

understand the essence of Buddhist philosophies: the impermanence of experiences, the detachment from outcomes, the acceptance of the present moment. And in this powerful fusion of rhythm and mindfulness, you find a unique pathway to inner stillness, a percussive key that unlocks your inherent peace.

Invest in this rhythmic practice, for it offers you much more than an auditory experience. It offers you a harmonious balance, a mindful route to connect profoundly with your inner being, and ultimately, a rhythm that leads you towards enduring tranquility.

As you move forward, remember: If you're ever overwhelmed, take a respite with your rhythm, for even the simple act of focusing on a beat can usher in peace. Dive into the rhythm, free your spirit, and let the drumbeats guide you towards the tranquility, clarity, and mindfulness that you inherently possess.

Chapter 11. Concluding Cadence: Achieving Longevity in Inner Peace through Percussion

As we embark on the concluding cadence of this rhythmical journey, let us remember that the essence of slow, steady beats and the tranquil nature of Buddhist philosophy have served as our guides through a transformative process.

The resonant sound of the drum, for centuries, has been intimately associated with the vibrational therapies, enchanting not just our auditory senses but also touching our souls at a deeper level. This connection, when harnessed mindfully and with purpose, is an effective tool for achieving longevity in inner peace through percussion.

11.1. Discovery: Percussion and Inner Peace

The discovery of percussion instruments extends back into our primordial history, even before the formation of complex languages. It has communicated emotions, signified unity, and created rhythm in life. As human beings, we are intrinsically rhythmic. From our heartbeat to our breathing pattern, there exists a universal rhythm, an intimate connection with the cosmos perceived through the most primal percussive instrument, the human body.

Buddhist teachings also emphasize the significance of rhythm. The rhythmic chanting of sutras in monastic life, the ritualistic beat of the mokugyo during meditation, and the oscillation of prayer beads, all encapsulate rhythm's essence in the journey toward enlightenment.

Through harnessing the power of percussion, we endeavor to align our internal rhythm with the cosmic rhythm, facilitating our understanding and experience of life, and ultimately leading us to attain inner peace.

11.2. The Sound of Enlightenment

For the practitioners of Buddhism, the percussion instruments are not merely tools to produce sound. They are profound symbols of the central Buddhist teachings.

In the heated throes of life's suffering, the thunderous sound of the Dharma drum acts as a wake-up call, reminds us of the path we must continue onto enlightenment.

Another instrumental symbol is the wooden fish, used during rituals and chants to strike a rhythm. It is a reminder to be vigilant against the intoxications that can lead us away from our quest for peace and enlightenment.

The symbolic representation and the fundamental teachings embedded within the percussion instruments, highlights the intertwined relationship of Buddhism and percussion in achieving inner peace.

11.3. Mindful Drumming: Meditation in Motion

Mindful drumming can be looked at as meditation in motion. It demands both the physical act of creating beats and mental focus, forming a resonant connection between mind, body and spirit. As the drumstick hits the drum surface, it's not just a sound that emanates but an energy, a vibration.

In adopting rhythmic breathing and mirroring these patterns with our drumming, we create a physical manifestation of our inner energy. Intentional strikes and silence between each offer a journey into the depths of our beings, unveiling layers of emotions, unprocessed thoughts and internal harmony.

The synchronization of drum beats with our breath connects us to the present moment, encouraging mindfulness. This powerful blend of music and mindfulness aids in achieving longevity in inner peace.

11.4. Integrating Percussion into Daily Rituals

A significant approach to achieving longevity in inner peace through percussion is by incorporating it into our daily rituals.

Begin with creating a sacred space just for your musical pursuits. Choose a tranquil location where you can harmonize your breath with the subtle rhythms of your drumming. Allocate precise times in your daily routine for rhythmic meditation.

You can also create your own 'percussive mantras', rhythms that are personally meaningful and invite peace. Repeated drumming of these mantras can act as a meditative catalyst, helping you navigate toward the journey within.

The integration of percussion in daily routines can serve to firmly establish the state of inner peace, contributing to its longevity.

11.5. The Harmonious Cadence

The journey towards inner peace isn't a linear path but a cyclical rhythm, oscillating between knowledge acquisition, self-discovery, mindful practice, and enlightenment. The conclusion isn't an end, but another beginning, another beat in the grand rhythm of life.

In this rhythmic voyage of self-discovery and serenity, we have found a resonant alignment in the spectrum of Buddhist philosophy and the rhythm of our being through percussion. We have picked up the drumsticks and followed the beat of our hearts, curated mindful practices and built powerful mantras. At the end of this phrase, we're ready to perceive the melody in the silence, the rhythm in the chaos, and peace within the resonance.

The beat goes on as does our relentless pursuit of peace. The melodic music of life, embedded with beats of joy, hardships, love, and losses, invariably progresses. With the drum in one hand and enlightenment in the other, we'll maintain the cadence, navigating rhythmically towards a serene symphony of inner peace that reverberates with time and the universe. We've learned that every beat matters just like every moment. So as you immerse in the rhythms of your music or life, remember to remain mindful, attuned, and at peace. Let the journey continue and let the drums roll on.

May the rhythms guide your way to eternal peace, and may the drum forever resonate with your enlightened spirit!